Mastering The 21 Immutable Principles Of Brazilian Jiu-Jitsu

by

Paulo Guillobel

Acknowledgements

First, I'd like to thank my parents, Cida and Jose Paulo, for their love and support through all of my life's endeavors. I'd surely like to thank the five jiu-jitsu masters that have had the most influence in my life and in my jiu-jitsu, Jorge Pereira, Rigan and Jean Jacques Machado, Saulo Ribeiro and Xande Ribeiro, for sharing their amazing knowledge, believing in me, and molding me into the Black Belt I am today.

I'd also like to thank all my students and training partners for supporting me, being there when needed, and helping me grow as a teacher (and as a student). Thanks to my student, Dirk Anderson, for reviewing this book and correcting my second language misspellings.

Special thanks to the Gracie Family for sharing this amazing martial art style with the world.

Table of Contents

Introduction

> **❝Learning through practice is like pushing a cart up hill: if you slack off, it will slip backwards.❞**
>
> —A Japanese proverb

After many years as a student and instructor of Brazilian jiu-jitsu (BJJ), I've realized that what distinguishes a true expert in BJJ from all others is not the number of new techniques he can show (or execute) but a complete understanding of the basic principles of the art.

A good number of instructors are now far more focused on showing new trends, forgetting the importance of teaching students the major principles mentioned above. This can create a watering down effect for future generations, diminishing the value of what is considered the most efficient self-defense style ever created.

New techniques are important as BJJ is always evolving. A good instructor should provide his students the opportunity to stay current on new trends. The problem? Over the years, I've witnessed countless BJJ fighters applying interesting, new, ever-changing techniques while lacking a keen understanding of the most fundamental Brazilian Jiu-jitsu principles and concepts. Remember, BJJ principles and concepts remain changeless over time. Together they constitute the core of our art.

I've written this book to provide the most important principles any BJJ fighter should know. Understanding and following these principles will dramatically improve your BJJ game and develop you into a more complete Black Belt one day.

I can confidently say that there are 21 immutable principles I've learned along my Brazilian jiu-jitsu journey. These principles are the keystones in the 'game' of the majority of the dominant BJJ champions in our history. They represent the basis of my accomplishments and my students' accomplishments as well. I believe Master Rickson Gracie calls them "the invisible techniques"; I call them the *21 Immutable Principles of Brazilian Jiu-Jitsu.*

Why the term *Immutable Principles of Brazilian jiu-jitsu*? One of the definitions of principle is: *a basic belief, theory, or rule that has a major influence on the way in which something is done*; and the definition of Immutable is: *Impossible to change*. So, putting them together we get: *the unchangeable basic belief, theory, or rule that has a major influence on the way in which something (Brazilian jiu-jitsu) is done.*

The conclusion is that the trend techniques will always change and evolve, but these *immutable principles* will always stay the same, and they will help you better understand any BJJ technique, whether it is long-established or the newest trend.

Why should you read what I have to say?

My connection with Brazilian jiu-jitsu began in Rio in 1988 when I walked into my first class with Master Jorge Pereira (now a Grand Master). Instantly drawn to the sport, I dedicated my life to mastering it and to excelling as a competitor and a fighter. Since then, I have won many major national and international tournaments, including five Pan American Championships (Adult & Masters) and two World Masters No-Gi Championships, among others.

Focused teaching of the fundamentals has resulted in competitive success for my students, producing numerous Pan American Champions, National Champions, and World Champions. I attribute my achievements and those of my students to these *principles*, and to the great BJJ instructors who reinforced these principles as I developed my 'game'.

I wrote this book to pass on these principles to generations to come. It took me almost two years of carefully analyzing every thought that I had about this subject to finally compile all the ideas I discuss in this book.

How did I learn these Immutable Principles?

I was fortunate to train under several amazing and legendary Brazilian jiu-jitsu masters (Saulo and Xande Ribeiro, Jean Jacques, Rigan Machado, and Jorge Pereira), and also had the opportunity to train with other BJJ masters, such as Royler Gracie, Carlos Gracie Jr., and many others. I've learned a considerable amount from listening to what they had to say and observing what they did. But teaching was what really opened my mind to research further into the core basics. It forced me to find the right answers to my students' questions and also to identify the best ways to properly explain those answers to them.

In my life, I've had the capacity to wear both the instructor's hat and the student's hat. I believe we are all lifelong students and the day we stop learning is the day we give up on life. Today, I am blessed to train under Saulo Ribeiro, an amazing instructor. Saulo deserves credit for advancing my understanding of many of these principles I now present to you.

What are these 21 Fundamental Principles of BJJ?

Below are the titles I've given each principle. I've dedicated a chapter to each concept, providing thorough explanations so you can take full advantage and, hopefully, adapt them to your jiu-jitsu game.

1. The 7 P's of Guard Passing

2. The Chess Game Analogy

3. The Wet Rug Analogy

4. The Zen Stage

5. Flow Like Water

6. The Braveheart Analogy

7. The American Football Analogy

8. The Leak and the Bucket of Water

9. Avoid Overreaching

Note: When you start reading the chapters of this book, you will notice that I refer to our opponent or training partner as *he* instead of he/she. I do not mean this as a slight to women, only as a convenience.

I don't know the current level of your Brazilian jiu-jitsu game, so I strongly suggest that you read this book more than once as you develop your skills. There may be principles in this book that you are not ready to understand yet, but if you consistently reference these concepts as your BJJ game evolves, you will soon connect to ideas you didn't connect with previously. That being said, let's begin....

Chapter 1

The 7 P's of Guard Passing

> **In the opening a master should play like a book, in the mid-game he should play like a magician, in the ending he should play like a machine.**
>
> —Rudolph Spielmann, Chess Master

The idea of this principle was born in a phone conversation with a Black Belt friend of mine, Joe Savoian. Joe asked my opinion on a teaching approach to help his students better remember the most important concepts of guard passing.

After identifying the '4 P's of Passing the Guard', Joe asked if I thought his list was complete.

His '4 P's of Passing the Guard' were:

1. Patience

2. Pressure

3. Persistence

4. Posture

I thought this was a great idea, so I started to think what other P's might be missing. As I watched my students work their guard passing at my school, the idea finally popped into my head. At least 3 P's were missing – position, proper balance, and precision. So I transformed the '4 P's of Passing the Guard' into the '7 P's of Guard Passing':

1. Position

2. Posture

3. Pressure

4. Persistence

5. Patience

6. Proper Balance

7. Precision

In this chapter, I'll explain the P's in detail, so you can understand and apply them ALL the next time you are passing someone's guard. Notice that I capitalized the word ALL because if you don't use all of the 7 P's together, then you will risk not achieving the guard pass.

POSITION

Position is being at the right place, in the right way, and at the right time.

It's easier said than done, but if you know where you want to be while passing somebody's guard, getting there should be one of your main goals.

Every technique has what I call **'the first step'**. When we learn a Brazilian jiu-jitsu technique, or that of any other martial art, the instructor breaks it down into many steps, starting from a certain position referred to as the 'first step'.

This first step starts the sequence of moves necessary to properly complete the technique. For example, it can take us to a single technique, like the *Toreada Pass*, or to a sequence of technical combinations like combining an *arm-bar* with *choke* from the mount **(see Figure 1)**.

After the first step obviously comes the second, but effectively progressing to the second step demands that you properly execute the first. This sounds extremely simple and redundant, but experience has convinced me that many people want to finish the sequence without properly performing the *first step*. In Figure 1, I have my legs ready to throw an *arm-bar* and my hands ready to choke my partner. From here, I can choose which technique to apply, depending upon my partner's reaction.

Once you know exactly where and how your first position (first step) starts, all that remains is to pursue the proper position to launch your solo attack or sequence of attacks. If you are not continuously pursuing the proper starting point for your techniques (which is the

Figure 1

first step in your sequence of moves to correctly complete your chosen technique), you cannot effectively start to attack or defend against your opponent. This is only one of the many examples of how important position is in BJJ. When you are passing your opponent's guard, you should always position yourself in a way that optimizes your balance since you are applying a certain amount of pressure with your weight. Also, you have to look for the proper angle in order to maximize your weight in

Figure 2

continually seeking to fatigue your opponent.

Figure 2 provides an example of position in the open guard. In the picture, my right shin is directly behind one of my partner's knees while my other leg is slightly behind my front leg. My hips are almost above my partner's hips and my elbows are in between my partner's legs.

Every detail of this position must be established before proceeding. This is *the first step* in a sequence of attacks with the objective of passing my opponent's guard. I won't focus on the complex details of my position because this book is about principles, not techniques. However, I will provide explanations in order to emphasize the importance of your position.

My right shin is behind the knee for a couple reasons: 1) to apply pressure on his leg (which wears my opponent out and helps me to flatten his hips), and 2) it breaks the angle of specific guards like De la Riva, Butterfly, and others. My other leg is slightly behind, providing my front leg with more leverage. My elbows are positioned between his legs where they are safe from *omoplatas* (and other attacks), and my hips are placed close to his hips, eliminating the space my opponent needs to set up his open guard.

Finding the right position is crucial when it comes to passing your opponent's guard, and this also applies to every other jiu-jitsu situation you will face. It is important to have a good reason for choosing a particular position at any stage in a fight. But position is not everything, which brings us to the second 'P'.

POSTURE

Some will say that posture is part of good position. Well, if you achieved good position while attempting to pass your opponent's guard, you were probably using good posture. But you can also have good posture without having good position, and good position without being in good posture.

Figure 3

Maintaining proper posture while passing your opponent's guard gives you a good start towards reaching your pass without falling into easy submissions or sweeps.

Good ways to make sure you have the right posture include never leaning too much or too little, and keeping a proper balance between your head and hips. **In Figure 3**, I show an example of using bad posture while attempting to pass my opponent's *spider guard*. My head is down and my legs are positioned behind my upper body, making it really easy for my opponent to catch me in a *triangle submission.*

On the other hand, in **Figure 4**, my head is held high and I am putting my shin slightly in front of my upper body, applying pressure on one of his legs. This defends against my opponent's triangle attacks.

Figure 4

Figure 5 shows another example of good posture in closed guard. Notice

Figure 5

that my body has the shape of a pyramid, which provides stable balance.

In summary, good posture improves overall balance and offers an effective defense against submissions like chokes and triangles. So good posture and position are two very important fundamentals to have while passing someone's guard, but without pressure you are not optimizing either.

PRESSURE

There are a few different ways to apply pressure on your opponent while passing his guard. I will mention the most important ones in this chapter; remember that you will always achieve better results when they are used in combination.

Weight Pressure

Gravity can be your best friend or your worst enemy when you are on top in a fight.

It's really hard to pass a good guard without applying weight pressure, but too much weight pressure directed on the wrong spot can get you swept or submitted. When passing someone's guard, you have a weight advantage because he is unable to utilize his own weight against you – and you definitely can use yours against him.

I like to tell my students that gravity can be their best friend or their worst enemy. Why? Because proper use of your weight while passing guard will wear your opponent out by forcing him to always push against your weight. I can't stress the importance of maximizing your weight enough. Always search for the best angles to force your opponent to use up his strength.

> **A little warning here:** if you use your weight incorrectly, your opponent can take advantage by using your weight against you. If you lean too much or lean the wrong direction, you are susceptible to being swept or submitted.

There are ways to maximize your weight pressure when you are passing guard. I'll explain further in future chapters.

Speed Pressure

Pressure can also be applied by using your speed to switch positions or techniques. However, you must be conditioned to move fast and also be able to maintain the necessary pace until you achieve your goal, which in this case is to create fatigue in your opponent (or force him to make a mistake).

By moving quickly from one position (or technique) to another, you can push the pace of the fight to a level your opponent won't be able match. But you must have more stamina than your partner; otherwise this strategy will backfire!

If you are fast and know when to use your speed, your opponent may struggle to keep up. If he starts to slow down, multiple opportunities will open up for you to pass his guard. Very few people know how to fight properly at a faster pace. If you force your partner to fight under these conditions, you will see more mistakes and potentially break an opponent's will.

While pushing the pace, you must not forget to breathe properly. Many BJJ fighters push the pace of the fight like they are sprinting underwater. By the time the sprint is over, they are exhausted, which gives their opponent a new opportunity to turn the fight to their advantage.

Only use speed when you know for sure that your opponent won't be able to keep up with you, and ALWAYS save most of your energy for when you really need it.

How to Improve Your Speed

A great way to improve your speed is by doing sprint drills, where you drill the same technique over and over, adding more speed each time. You can also count how many repetitions of a particular technique you can do within a certain time frame, and set a goal to increase it each round.

While performing BJJ sprint drills, it's very important not to lose focus on executing the technique correctly. In addition to BJJ drills, you can also cross-train. Try sprinting while running, cycling or swimming.

PERSISTENCE

Well, persistence is self-explanatory but often forgotten when BJJ fighters are passing an opponent's guard. For instance, imagine you are repeatedly trying to pass the guard with no success...so you give up and go for a *foot lock*. Using this approach, you will NEVER master guard passing because rather than finding ways to pass your opponent's guard, you relented and switched course to another technique.

I'm not saying that you should never go for a foot lock while attempting to pass your opponent's guard, but if your goal is to learn guard passing, that should be your sole focus until you succeed.

By persisting in passing someone's guard, you will eventually reap the benefits of your effort. A champion learns from both successes and mistakes, but never by giving up.

Generally, you will need to wear your opponent out to pass his *guard*, and persistence is a key factor in doing that.

I often see people put a lot of pressure on their opponents by using good *guard passing* transitions, only to give up a second before they would have completed their pass. Most of the time, passing a good guard is like boiling food – if you stop cooking the food moments before it would have started boiling, you will not get the same result as you would have if you had waited until it reached the *boiling point*.

PATIENCE

Having a lack of patience when passing someone's guard can really put you at risk. How?

In a Brazilian jiu-jitsu match, timing is everything. You CAN'T lose your cool and start making moves at the wrong time. When this happens, you give your opponent a great opportunity to surprise you by making his own move.

Many BJJ experts, including myself, will wait for the opponent to make a mistake, and then capitalize on it. This is the easiest way to get ahead in a fight. Also, if you are doing everything right during the fight, why rush into moves (and force positions) that are not there to be taken?

Everyone eventually makes one wrong move, opening them up to be attacked during a fight. When you can't see a way to progress in a fight on your own, wait for a mistake to present itself – then be ready to capitalize on it.

I have an interesting story about patience.

I was trying to pass Saulo Ribeiro's guard (if you don't know who he is, please Google him), and I noticed he wasn't attacking me. He was just reacting to my moves, trying to catch my mistakes. A light bulb went on in my head; I thought, "I will not move either. Let's see who moves first." So I kept my position without moving an inch. Guess what happened? We stayed in the same position for several minutes, watching each other's face until I couldn't take it anymore and moved. The split second that I was making my move, he moved faster – almost as if he had initiated the move – and he ended up sweeping me. I always wonder how much longer he would have waited for me to make the first move. That was a very useful lesson in patience.

PROPER BALANCE

This is another very important 'P'. Our balance on top is what keeps us on top while passing an opponent's Guard.

While in the process of passing your opponent's guard, you will have to defend many submission attacks and/or sweep attempts. Good position on top with proper balance is your 'tool' for surviving these attacks so that you can continue marching toward your objective of passing the guard.

Maintaining good balance requires consistent focus while also concentrating on your opponent's position to gain feedback for reading his next move. For that you'll have to observe his moves closely. Watch where he is trying to take you (by him making it easier for you) and where he is making it harder for you to go (his weak side). Also analyze his hooks, grips and the position of his body.

Another important principle of good balance is your head position. The head is the heaviest part of the body. There are things to pay attention to when balancing your head (along with the rest of your body) on top of your opponent.

For example: If most of your body is moving to the left, you should lean your head to the right to keep your weight centered on top of your opponent.

Figure 6

In most cases when guard passing, I try to keep a 45 degree angle to my opponent's body. (**See Figure 6** and/or watch your FREE BONUS video tutorial by going to **www.21BJJ Principles.com**)

Always ask yourself these important questions: Am I leaning too much in a certain direction? If I step this foot here, or put my hand there, or make this grip, or drop my knee, will I lose my balance?

If the answer to either of the questions above is "yes", you are about to make the wrong move and lose your balance.

PRECISION

Precision is the quality or state of being precise – exactness. It is reflected in the degree of refinement with which an operation (technique) is performed.

You can master all the P's above, but without taking the right action at the right time and in the right way, you won't be able to pass your opponent's guard at will.

Precision relies on both the timing of execution and the action being executed. You must know when your opponent is giving you something, what he is giving you, and the proper technique to immediately use against him in that moment.

Precision is mastered only through repetition of action – both while drilling and during real matches. Don't get discouraged. As you gain experience through your training, an increasing number of situations in which you can utilize the techniques you've learned will become clear in your mind. Your goal is to identify those situations and then properly execute your techniques at the right time. Timing is everything!

Chapter 2

The Chess Game Analogy

66 I do not play chess–I fight at chess. Therefore I willingly combine the tactical with the strategic, the fantastic with the scientific, the combinative with the positional, and I aim to respond to the demands of each given position ... 99

—Alexander Alekhine, Chess Master

One of my hobbies is playing chess. I find that the many similarities between chess and jiu-jitsu are extremely helpful in my BJJ game. I'll go over the most important ones with you.

Controlling the Center of The Board

66 If the defender is forced to give up the center, then every possible attack follows almost of itself. 99

—Siegbert Tarrasch (chess player)

One day I was reading a really good chess book when I came across a paragraph that stated that one of the best ways to take control of a chess game is by controlling the center of the board. I had always thought the best way to win a chess match was by chasing the checkmate. But, according to this book, good position is a key element to achieving the checkmate.

But what does this have to do with Brazilian jiu-jitsu?

What is our opponent's 'center of the board'? I would say the hips, right? Every single move we make in jiu-jitsu involves moving our hips. Without moving our hips, we really can't go anywhere.

Most people think that ONLY chasing the submission (a position in which we force our opponent to quit) is the best strategy to win a BJJ match – notice that I capitalized ONLY. This is because we must always keep at least one eye on submission possibilities. Personally, I believe that controlling our opponent's 'center of the board' by keeping the board (hips) in a flat, restricted position (preventing them from moving at will) is the best path to securing a submission.

And here is why...

If you have good control over your opponent's body, you will have many more chances to get the submission because your opponent isn't going anywhere but into your 'trap'. However, going for submissions only, without thinking about controlling the hips, may lead you to a series of failed attempts, giving your opponent chances to move and counterattack. The best way to control our opponent's body is by developing ways to control his hips.

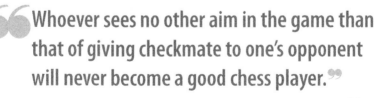

Whoever sees no other aim in the game than that of giving checkmate to one's opponent will never become a good chess player.

——Max Euwe

So how have these principles changed my BJJ game?

When I learned this principle, I began shifting my focus to my opponent's hips, working to flatten him on the mat at all times. This focus improved my game dramatically! Instead of thinking about my array of techniques (and how to use them), I began to strategically analyze the position of my opponent's hips and develop ways to keep them flat. This new paradigm helped me to neutralize both my opponent's attacks and counterattacks, opening more opportunities for the submission. Observing my opponent's hips also helped me to better understand the strengths and weaknesses in my positioning.

The Checkmate

Winning a chess match requires that you *checkmate* an opponent. We call *checkmate* (!) when our opponent has his king – the most important piece in the game – trapped in an indefensible position. In BJJ, our *checkmate* is the submission.

Submission is achieved when your opponent is placed in a situation he can't escape from without being choked or suffering a broken bone or ligament tear – when the opponent will lose regardless of his attempts to counter or escape.

Ultimately, we want to put our opponent in a *submission* hold. When we combine a variety of submission techniques while controlling our opponent, we are using the most secure way to reach our final goal (make our opponent quit), but that is not the only way.

You can also be a *submission-driven fighter,* not caring too much for maintaining control positions but always aware of opportunities to submit your opponent. *Submission-driven fighters* utilize many good positions (and controls) throughout the fight, but they are most feared by their opponents because of their ability to get *submissions* from every angle.

Tip: We usually improve the part of our *game* that we are most focused on. If you focus your BJJ strategy on submissions, you will eventually become really good at them.

Thinking Ahead

As with chess, in jiu-jitsu you must be at least <u>three moves</u> ahead of your partner to win. You must foresee all possible reactions available to your opponent based on his position and his intention in the fight.

How can you be Three or More Moves Ahead of your Opponent?

> The plan in a game of chess is the sum total of successive strategic operations which are each carried out according to separate ideas arising from the demands of the position.
>
> —Alexander Kotov

One way is through a lot of practice and by having a game plan that places you in similar circumstances as often as possible with different partners of varying levels. This is important because partners react differently to the same set of conditions. You will learn to anticipate and identify a range of possible reactions to the same position.

Another way is by using combinations.

> The scheme of a game is played on positional lines; the decision of it, as a rule, is effected by combinations.
>
> —Richard Reti

A combination is having more than one option for each position. Here are a couple examples:

You can attack your partner's neck when you really want your partner to move his head away in order to expose his arm for an arm-lock; or pulling him forward and then sweeping him backwards. There are many examples of combinations. I'll talk more about them in the FREE tutorial videos included with this book (to watch go to www.21BJJPrinciples.com)

> **Note:** Acknowledging the fact that your opponent will always want to react against your moves *must* be used as a strategy.

Practical example: when you want your opponent to move forward, push him away from you and then pull him forward. See what happens…once you understand how your partner will react, you'll be able to anticipate his next move.

The Value of the Positions

In the game of chess, pieces have varying levels of importance, and so do the positions in BJJ. For example: a pawn is worth less than a bishop, and a half guard is worth less than mount control. Make sense?

In chess, the king is the most important piece because if you lose your king, the game is lost. In BJJ, it is equally important to protect your arms, neck, wrists, legs, and feet; if they are exposed, you can lose the fight by getting any one of them caught in a *submission hold*.

The queen is the second most valuable piece in the chess game. Out of all of Brazilian jiu-jitsu's positions, mount and back control are the most valuable. Ask any Brazilian Jiu-Jitsu fighter (of any level) what type of control they really want to avoid – 9 out of 10 will say either mount or back control. That is how powerful (and valuable) these two positions are.

Side control and knee on the belly control are also very valuable positions, but not as valuable as the mount and back control. The guard, half guard, and guard passing are all important positions, but not as important as those mentioned above.

So how can you use this idea to your advantage?

In chess, a good strategy to catch one of your opponent's valuable pieces is to threaten two valuable pieces at the same time. Your opponent will always prioritize his most valuable pieces. When this happens, he gives you an opportunity to catch the less valuable piece (while he attempts to protect the more valuable).

Now let's bring this idea to our BJJ game. By understanding this principle (that every position has a level of importance in BJJ) you can use the same exact strategy, and guess what? It will work the same way it works in chess.

If you are not currently using this strategy in your game, this idea alone will completely transform your game. Let me give you some examples.

Let's review the three most valuable things you can achieve in BJJ: submission techniques (e.g., *arm-bar, choke, triangle, omoplata*, etc.) are the most valuable because they end the fight; or in the case of a street fight, they result in a serious injury to your opponent. Mount and back control are the second and third most valuable positions because they give you leverage toward the submission and, if well executed, are very hard to escape.

Following this principle, when I attempt to pass an opponent's guard, I often set my position to pressure my opponent into defending the mount. While my opponent is desperately focused defending the mount, he will often leave an opening for a side control position (better for him than the mount), which helps me achieve my true goal of passing his guard. Remember my chess analogy – positions vary in level of importance.

Another example: defending our guard. Continually attempting to submit your opponent from the bottom will provide opportunities to sweep him, which will enable you to transition to the top position. This is because his main focus will be on defending the submission attempts. So, pursuing the submissions throughout a match will consistently distract your opponent's focus from other positions that you can pursue to gain advantage in your match.

Once you understand the hierarchy of BJJ positions (and those your opponent fears the most), your game will improve dramatically.

Chapter 3

The Wet Rug Analogy

"Man at his birth is supple and tender, but in death, he is rigid and hard. Thus, suppleness and tenderness accompany life, but rigidity and hardness accompany death."

—Lao-Tsu

Appling this principle correctly will completely change the way you control positions. The following chapter provides details.

Would it be more difficult to escape if I threw a 200-pound wet rug on top of you or a 200-pound piece of plywood? Which would take the most energy to push away? We can all agree that the wet rug will be harder to push away, right? Whenever I teach my students guard passing, side control and mount control, I emphasize this analogy. Remember, you can apply it any time you are on top of your opponent.

My point? When you are on top, you have the option to either relax your body or tense your body. You're using up your strength when you are too tense, and your body gets rigid. As a result, you are susceptible to being moved around (like the plywood). It is much more difficult for your opponent to move you when you remain relaxed (like trying to push a 200-pound wet rug). So the secret is to be as relaxed as possible, making an opponent's escape from your control considerably harder while conserving your energy during the match (crucial for your success).

Tip for Relaxing Your Body While Fighting (This tip not only applies to Brazilian jiu-jitsu but also to other activities you perform):

To better relax your body, you must control your breathing. Pay close attention to your breath during your training. Often you'll find yourself holding the air in your lungs as if underwater, which tenses your body.

Relax by making sure that you are exhaling air instead of holding it in. This helps to focus your breathing on the exhalation, not the inhalation.

If you are having a hard time controlling your breathing while training in BJJ, here's another good tip: make sounds when you are exhaling – almost like a whistling sound. This way you will hear your exhalation, making it easier to track.

Chapter 4

The Zen Stage

> **Technical knowledge is not enough. One must transcend techniques so that the art becomes an artless art, growing out of the unconscious.**
>
> —Daisetsu Suzuki

One day while reading a Zen Buddhism book, *Zen in the Art of Archery*, by Eugen Herringel, I came across a couple of ideas that can help us understand the art of Jiu-Jitsu. The book stressed the importance of repetition. Repeating one technique over and over for many years will result in 'thoughtless' execution of that technique. Your body's muscle memory will get to the point where it executes the technique like second nature.

Constant repetition (applied properly) will lead to perfecting a technique. At that point, your mind will reach a stage of emptiness (of thought) while executing the technique. This book refers to this occurrence as a 'Zen state of mind'.

The lesson learned? The more we drill a particular technique the right way, the more this technique becomes a habit. We are what we repetitively do – we are creatures of habit. To improve your jiu-jitsu game, you must improve your habits.

Notice in the paragraphs above that I used the words *right* and *proper*. The reason is because if you repeat a technique many times the wrong way, you will create a bad habit instead of a good one. That's why it is so important to have a good instructor that can point out your mistakes and help you correct them.

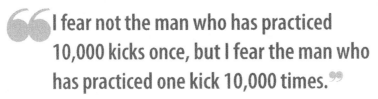

I fear not the man who has practiced 10,000 kicks once, but I fear the man who has practiced one kick 10,000 times.

—Bruce Lee

Chapter 5

Flow Like Water

> Water shapes its course according to the nature of the ground over which it flows; the soldier works out his victory in relation to the foe whom he is facing.
>
> —Sun Tzu

Another very interesting thing I found in this book: In Asia, the element that represents jiu-jitsu is water. Why?

Because water possesses the power to go through most anything, but <u>always</u> follows the path of least resistance by flowing and adapting its shape to the nature of its course.

Our jiu-jitsu should be the same; <u>always</u> look for the easiest way to apply techniques, regardless of your strength. And specifically adapt your Jiu-Jitsu game to each opponent.

BJJ fighters who fail to master this principle will always attempt to use strength to attack and defend, unaware of opportunities to conserve energy. Actions have consequences – you will become unnecessarily fatigued, placing yourself at risk to run out of energy and lose the match.

Methods for conserving strength are described in almost every chapter of this book. When you finish reading, it will be clear how to effectively apply this principle in your Jiu- Jitsu game.

Why save your energy? I'll discuss the importance of energy management further in following chapters.

Chapter 6

The *Braveheart* Analogy

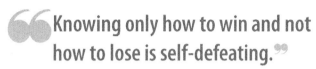**Knowing only how to win and not how to lose is self-defeating.**

—Tokugawa Ieyasu

Many people (ranging from white to black belts) begin BJJ matches by keeping their distance and trying to surprise their opponents with a fast jump or by running around them. In reality, they are avoiding the real fight.

This may work when you aren't facing a good opponent or when your opponent is unprepared. But when facing a good opponent who is prepared, it won't work the same way.

So what should you do instead? I always ask my students, "Have you watched the movie *Braveheart*?" Some say yes, and some say no. I tell those who say no to rent it after training (one of my favorite movies to watch, but I don't recommend it for kids, of course).

When you watch the battles in this movie, you don't see the warriors running around trying to avoid the enemy. You see them running straight toward each other into battle until the best wins.

They measure forces and skills, and then employ the appropriate techniques to overcome their enemy. Their developed sensory skills allow them to adapt to an enemy's strengths. They show courage by attacking, even when outnumbered, and face all attacks their enemy can muster.

In my opinion, the only way to master jiu-jitsu is by going right at your opponent's game and learning to neutralize it. You face a problem – now find the solution. You must identify their weaknesses and capitalize on them before they find yours. When you run from engaging directly in a Brazilian Jiu-Jitsu match, you are already showing a weakness – one that can feed your opponent's confidence.

Consciously work to find the proper way to distribute your weight by using gravity as an ally, not an enemy. Understand where your weight is being applied and why. Sense the optimal balance point when applying your weight and, conversely, whether your opponent has proper balance when applying his weight on you. You will only determine all of this through experience, and by facing your opponent's game instead of running from it.

Another important advantage of fighting the fight (and not avoiding it) is the opportunity it provides to wear your opponent out, instead of just tiring yourself.

For example, trying to avoid your opponent's guard by jumping around and looking for an easy way to pass only wears you out (far more than an opponent who maintains a sitting position). While lying down on the mat, your opponent is conserving energy when defending your jumps and crazy, poorly timed *toreadas* (**see Figure 7**).

Figure 7

Personally, I don't want to run out of gas before my opponent, do you?

Finding the right angles, the perfect leverage, and the right timing to optimize your power requires your complete commitment.

How will you find all these things by avoiding the fight? You won't. Please take a moment to consider the importance of this before you continue reading.

Here's another quote to motivate you:

> It is not the critic who counts: not the man who points out how the strong man stumbles or where the doer of deeds could have done better. The credit belongs to the man who is actually in the arena, whose face is marred by dust and sweat and blood, who strives valiantly, who errs and comes up short again and again, because there is no effort without error or shortcoming, but who knows the great enthusiasms, the great devotions, who spends himself for a worthy cause; who, at the best, knows, in the end, the triumph of high achievement, and who, at the worst, if he fails, at least he fails while daring greatly, so that his place shall never be with those cold and timid souls who knew neither victory nor defeat.
>
> —Theodore Roosevelt

Now do yourself a favor; the next time you train in BJJ, use the *Braveheart* principle without fear of losing. This is how your BJJ game will really improve. It might take some time getting used to, but believe me…it's worth it.

Chapter 7

The American Football Analogy

American Football?? Yup, Brazilian jiu-jitsu has a lot of similarities with American Football. I'm not talking about the physical contact or direct hits into the opponent's body. I'm talking about the core idea.

Let me explain…

American Football players fight for yards; BJJ fighters fight for inches.

Just as in American football, in BJJ you don't want to lose ground. Once you conquer that inch, the only thing you want is to conquer the next one until you have achieved the submission. I compare the touchdown with the submission. The hardest, most contested final yards in American football are referred to as 'the red zone', which I compare with control positions, such as mount, back, or even side control.

Football players don't move backwards without the clear intention of moving forward and gaining more yards toward their ultimate goal: a touchdown. In jiu-jitsu, even when moving backwards, your intention should be to find ways of moving forward into positions that enhance your chances of gaining a submission. The idea is to be prepared to take one step backwards to advance two steps forward.

Also in football, when one team gets the chance to initiate their offense and starts to attack, the other team tries to maintain its position. They must stop the opponent from moving forward, thereby neutralizing offensive plays until the defensive team regains the attack.

In Jiu-Jitsu, when you are not attacking, you are defending or counterattacking. Your defense must be flawless in order to neutralize your opponent's techniques, and to regain the offense from him.

A little observation here...

You can be in an attack position in Brazilian jiu-jitsu even when your body is at rest. Applying your weight forces an opponent to fight that weight off, and taps the opponent's strength, leaving him vulnerable to be attacked later in the fight.

Like American football, BJJ has offense strategies (combinations of techniques), which are the tools that allow you to move forward. Improving your position requires that you recognize when an opponent offers an opening and then exploit that opening to penetrate into the opponent's defense.

Chapter 8

The Leak and the Bucket

> **If you know the enemy and know yourself, you need not fear the result of a hundred battles. If you know yourself but not the enemy, for every victory gained you will also suffer a defeat. If you know neither the enemy nor yourself, you will succumb in every battle."**
>
> —Sun Tzu, The Art of War

This chapter will simplify your method of defending if you apply this principle in your game. It will also help you to find your own solutions, which is one key to a deeper understanding of the subtleties of any technique.

I recommend that you find a training partner or even your instructor (if he or she is available), and put this principle to work. This principle is among the many I've learned from Saulo Ribeiro. One day when we were training, I was having a hard time defending a certain technique when he stopped and said, "Paulo, if you have a lot of holes in your ceiling leaking water, under which leak would you put your first bucket?" The answer was obvious, "Under the biggest leak!" So a light bulb went on in my head, "The first thing I have to defend in any position is the one that gives my opponent the greatest leverage (which is the 'biggest leak')."

Once I understood this principle, life on the mat became much easier. Now before moving into any position, I identify the one detail that offers my opponent the greatest leverage against me and address it first. Only then can I begin the next movement in the sequence (recall the 'first step' I mentioned earlier?).

This detail can be a foot on my hips or a hand in my collar. It is any detail that gives my opponent the leverage he needs to properly execute a technique (his 'first step').

So, what is the second thing I must do when defending in any position? Identify the next 'big leak' of course (though at times the leak isn't obvious).

Now when you go back to your academy for your next training session, try to identify the 'leaks' in the techniques you want to improve your defense against. Then follow this recipe and see what happens.

This alone will help you to view (and rebuild) each technique with a more developed perspective.

To watch a video where I show how to find the biggest leak, go to www.21BJJPrinciples.com.

Chapter 9

Avoid Overreaching

>**Move swift as the Wind and closely-formed as the Wood. Attack like the Fire and be still as the Mountain.**
>
>—Sun Tzu

This principle is very simple, yet very hard to apply while in the midst of a fight.

For reasons I don't fully understand (maybe survival instinct), Brazilian jiu-jitsu practitioners frequently feel compelled to grab onto something that is almost out of their reach.

Maybe it happens when being smashed by our partner, and in an attempt to survive we reach out to the leg we expect our opponent will use against us. Or maybe when trying to pass the guard, we try to grab our opponent's far arm, thinking it will disrupt his leverage. When overreaching from the top, our balance is compromised, giving our opponent a good chance to isolate our arms from our core. Both situations can quickly put you in a bad spot in a fight. The more our body is used as a whole (closely-formed), the stronger our technique.

When overreaching from the bottom, we also expose parts of our body. This empowers a good opponent with a larger variety of potential attacks.

There are two major ways students overreach:

1. Reaching for a part of our opponent's body that is too far away from our core or center of balance; and
2. Grabbing some part of our opponent's body within our reach, but maintaining the grip while the opponent is moving this particular part of his body away from our core (or center of balance).

Both expose your arms to an opponent's attacks. One arm fighting against the opponent's two arms (or legs, etc.) can neither properly attack nor defend during a BJJ match.

> **Black Belt Tip:** Make sure that your arms are always close to your core, so you can use your core to protect your arms if it is necessary.

Chapter 10

The Fortress Analogy

> **Engage people with what they expect; it is what they are able to discern and confirms their projections. It settles them into predictable patterns of response, occupying their minds while you wait for the extraordinary moment — that which they cannot anticipate.**
>
> —Sun Tzu

Master Rillion Gracie brought the fortress analogy to my attention. He compared our Brazilian jiu-jitsu guard with a fortress. This immediately resonated with me; I now consistently defend my guard with this in mind.

Our feet, legs, hips, arms and hands work as our *fortress* walls – and its warriors. The objective of our guard is to defend from any form of attack, block our opponent from penetrating through our defenses, and attack back (mostly through using *submissions* and *sweeps)*. Guard is what distinguishes Brazilian (or Gracie) jiu-jitsu from any other form of martial arts ever created.

There are two other advantages of using our *BJJ guard:* 1) because our back is against the ground (most of the time), the fighter using his guard can rest his body there; and 2) if his guard is sharp, he can use his opponent's own weight against him.

Let's start with...

THE CLOSED GUARD

If guard is our fortress, closed guard would be a fortress with its gates closed to the enemy. This is a very important concept because when defending guard, people often go straight to the open guard, skipping a very important aspect of their guard. The closed guard provides unique advantages against an opponent's attack.

Let me give you a couple of good reasons to train your closed guard:

1. You can wear your partner down by breaking his grips and posture; therefore, if he does open your guard, he'll have less energy than if he had skipped this step;
2. It's a great position with a variety of options to attack your opponent for the submission or a sweep;
3. Many jiu-jitsu practitioners don't know how to open a good guard properly. If you do a good job there, you won't even need to open your guard; and
4. If you fail at all of your submission and sweep attempts, you still have your open guard to defend your fortress.

When the guard is opened, the gates are opened. Now your opponent's 'army' is battling directly with your 'army'. It is less secure than closed guard, but if you have a good 'army' (game), you still can succeed at defeating your opponent's attack.

THE OPEN GUARD

When your legs are not crossed behind your opponent's back, your guard is opened.

The Open Guard Objectives:
- Control the distance
- Disrupt opponent's balance
- Use action & reaction – see chapter 11
- Move hips

- Defend against attacks of any form
- Attack with submissions, sweeps and strikes (for self-defense only)

Controlling the Distance

When defending the *open guard*, you must never let your opponent get in a good position to attack. Jiu-Jitsu is, above all, a form of self-defense, and if your opponent is close enough and balanced enough to attack (e.g., strike) from the top, you are giving him the advantage.

Also, from a grappling point of view, if your opponent is putting you in an uncomfortable position by using his weight pressure, and you are allowing him to move forward towards *side, mount or back control* – you are failing in defending your guard.

When executing your open guard, you must control the distance between you and your opponent at all times. You either want your opponent far enough away so that you can stablish your guard (any style you prefer) or over your body where his balance can be disrupted with your moves.

Disrupting Your Opponent's Balance

Chapter 21 is about the importance of a good base and the correlation between base and balance. If maintaining good balance on top is so important, then it is vital that you don't allow your opponent to establish balance at will.

To disrupt your opponent's balance by using our open guard, you have to use your limbs to either make your opponent move against his will or get yourself moved out of the way. To move your opponent, you must use a combination of your limbs (e.g., feet, legs, hips, hands, and arms) to either pull or push him. The *key* to moving yourself out of the way is to move your hips (there are many drills showing how to move your hips on the bottom – *hip escape* is a good example).

Another great way to disrupt your opponent's balance is by using *the Principle of Action & Reaction.*

Using the Principle of Action and Reaction

We're going to talk more about this principle in the next chapter, but I'll give you the basic idea of how to apply it when implementing your open guard.

Use your opponent's own movement against him. Pay close attention to which direction your opponent's head is moving towards, then use your body to push or pull him to the same direction. This will generate unexpected energy to propel your opponent beyond the point he intended to go, therefore forcing him to lose his balance.

To watch a video where I demonstrate this principle, go to **www.21BJJPrinciples.com**

Moving Your Hips

When on the bottom, you have to move your hips to switch angles. If you stay static, you'll become an easy target. Moving our legs and arms are not enough to perform a good Open Guard. Unlike being on top, when using your Guard, you cannot walk, run, or jump, as a result, you're left with moving your hips to defend and attack.

There are many drills that help you develop a good hip mobility from the *bottom*. I show some good ones at the tutorial video series of this book (readers of this book have free access to these videos, just go to: **www.21BJJprinciples.com**). Most importantly, I want you to focus consistently on moving your hips, changing angles, when performing your Open Guard.

Defending Against Attacks of Any Form

If you understand the fundamental open guard principles I mentioned before, defending against attacks will be a little easier. We can't forget that BJJ is a form of self-defense; consequently, at all times we should be thinking about defending from submissions, strikes, and guard passes.

Attacking with Submissions, Sweeps and Strikes (Yep, I said Strikes)

The open guard is not utilized solely for defense; it's also a great place to attack back with submissions, sweeps and also strikes.

"Strikes?!" Well…Brazilian jiu-jitsu is not only what you see at tournaments. Beyond that there are a large number of moves that have been developed to defend you from other martial art styles or ordinary brawlers. The best strikes from your open guard are the ones that use your heels (bottom or back) (**see Figure 8 and 9**).

Figure 8

Figure 9

Likewise, your open guard provides you an array of submissions and sweeps (which you can combine together).

In summary, you have to make the best of your *fortress* by never allowing an opponent to pass it or beat you from it. When your opponent passes your guard, he invades the fortress; he is inside and you are fighting to survive.

So now that you know this, why not work on your guard so that you can make it even harder for your opponent to conquer your *fortress*?

Chapter 11

Action and Reaction

"When the enemy is relaxed, make them toil. When full, starve them. When settled, make them move."

—Sun Tzu

As we know, for every action there is a reaction. That not only applies to Jiu-Jitsu; it is also the essence of life.

jiu-jitsu is about using the least amount of effort to achieve the maximum result, and using the principle of *action and reaction* is the best approach to be successful.

What is *action*? In this case, action is the movement you (or your opponent) make with your body. My saying for action and reaction is: Nothing happens until something happens. The fight only starts when somebody moves (action), and from this point forward, it is all about action and reaction.

What is *reaction* then? The dictionary defines reaction as *your ability to think and act quickly in a difficult or dangerous situation.*

So action can be an opponent making a move against you (or the other way around)—and you responding by thinking and acting quickly upon his move (defending it or counterattacking it). Now that you know the definitions of action and reaction, how can you use this as a strategy to enhance your leverage and conserve your energy?

Your goal when making a move to attack your partner is to be aware of his array of possible defensive reactions. When you understand the most probable defensive reactions your opponent can potentially make, you are arming yourself to use his reaction as an opportunity to gain more power (leverage), and to plan your next move.

This is a common strategy in jiu-jitsu: force the opponent to react, and then take advantage of his reaction. Reacting quickly when he acts allows you to utilize his energy to leverage your moves. Let me give you some examples. For instance, when you push your opponent, he will instinctively push back with the same (or increased) intensity. Not surprisingly, this applies to pulling too.

So, if you want to pull your opponent forward, push him backwards first. As he reacts by pushing against your push, pull him – adding his energy to yours. This is how we expend the least amount of energy to pull him forward. Again, this approach can be applied whenever you are trying to lead your opponent into a different position.

When you want to sweep an opponent to your left, move him to your right first to compromise his balance and see what happens. A lot of people call the principle of action and reaction 'bait & trap'. The idea is to lure your opponent into reacting the way you want, not the other way around.

You can use the principle of *action and reaction* by reacting quickly to your opponent's move. For instance, if he is moving his body forward with x amount of speed, you will increase his speed if you pull him to the same direction and possibly force him to lose some of his balance. Another example: anticipate his next move and then use his momentum to leverage your next move.

There are literally thousands of ways to use the principle of *action and reaction* to facilitate your attacks and defenses. The purpose of this book is not to present them all. Instead, my goal is to develop your understanding of this principle so you'll know how to use it when fighting your opponents.

If you're not using 'action and reaction' in your Jiu-Jitsu game, go to your academy and start using it today. I guarantee you will see an improvement in your game.

For additional examples of *action & reaction* go to

www.21BJJPrinciples.com and watch the complementary video for this chapter.

Being Counterproductive

We are counterproductive when we make moves that get results opposite of those we intend to achieve. This is one of the major mistakes Brazilian jiu-jitsu students make. Knowing this from the beginning will save you a lot of energy, and improve your game more quickly.

I'll give a very basic example so you can get the idea. Imagine a situation where your opponent mounts you and you want to escape. The reason you want to escape is to avoid being caught in a submission (*armbar* for instance). Then, in attempting to escape, you push his chest up (or to the side), stretching your arm and leaving it exposed to an armbar attack. This is a typical example of counter-productivity. You want something, but your body is sending a different message that does not resonate with what you want.

Chapter 12

The Anatomy principle

Having a little knowledge of human anatomy will be extremely beneficial to your BJJ game.

When I started training in Brazilian Jiu-Jitsu back in 1988, I was a young boy with no knowledge of any martial art style. I had no understanding of joint manipulation, pressure points, base, balance, weight distribution, leverage, etc. These words were like *Greek* to me.

The great teaching skills of my first instructor (Sensei Jorge Pereira) opened my mind to the concept of anatomy. Fascinated, I was hungry to learn how to utilize my anatomy (while exploiting my partner's anatomy) in my own Brazilian jiu-jitsu game.

The first thing I learned was that it is easier (and more powerful) to pull or push certain parts of my opponent's body than others. Grabbing the wrist, for example, was easier and more effective than grabbing the biceps. Pushing the hips was way more effective than pushing the chest, and so on.

The second thing I learned was that my moves have to correspond with what I want to achieve. Let me explain this further, as I see a lot of people still making this mistake.

Let's say you're in an opponent's side control and you are trying to escape from the bottom by hugging your opponent. Your mind might be thinking, "I want to get out of here!" but when hugging your opponent, your body is suggesting otherwise.

When you hug someone, do you do it because you want to move him (or her) away? Isn't it to keep them close? Think about it.

Let's imagine again that you want to escape from side control (for example, he is smashing you against the ground) – you need to create some room between you and your opponent. Instead of having your arms ready between you and your opponent to push him at the appropriate moment **(Figure 10)**, you hug and pull your opponent against you, helping him to smash you even more **(Figure 11)**. It doesn't make sense, but it happens a lot.

Figure 10

Figure 11

So, in this chapter I will go over some of the principles I've learned through great instruction and my personal experiments on this concept. I'll also give ideas on how to properly use your opponent's body in conjunction with yours to maximize your results.

Let's start with…

THE WRIST

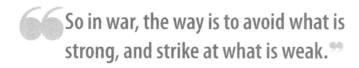

So in war, the way is to avoid what is strong, and strike at what is weak.

—Sun Tzu

In Brazilian jiu-jitsu we aren't allowed to submit our opponent by attacking their fingers. This submission is only used in specific self-defense cases but not in tournaments and regular training sessions (to avoid injury).

The wrist is the next weakest joint that is legal to attack. The most common way to take advantage of your opponent's wrist is by attacking with the wrist lock. This technique is considered 'cheap' in many BJJ schools because it is very hard to tap out your partner without injuring him. However, it is legal and not difficult to get **(see Figure 12)**.

Figure 12

> **Note:** Because you don't need to be an expert in Jiu-Jitsu to be good at wrist locks, a lot of people focus exclusively on them, straying from the path of the core basics.

Here are a few of the downsides of ONLY going for wrist locks:

1. You will probably hurt all of your teammates, and they'll soon hate to train with you;

2. Because you are hurting everyone, you will have fewer partners to train with and anger your instructor;

3. You will lose focus on more important fundamental techniques and basics. For example, how to pass guard, apply takedowns, defend your guard, etc. – all because you were caught up on submitting people only by wrist locking them;

4. Even if you attack the wrist slowly, your partners might still be hurt because out of pride they might only tap out when they feel the pain (and then it is too late for them); and

5. Your partners eventually will figure out your strategy, and they'll counter it more easily.

Okay, now that you know all the negatives associated with wrist locking people, I strongly suggest that you prioritize your BJJ basics, and only incorporate the wrist lock into your 'arsenal' when you get really good at them.

The Benefits of Controlling the Wrist

There are also many benefits in using your opponent's wrist against him. You can control your opponent's wrist when you are doing any kind of arm-bar. By grabbing or pulling the wrist, you are applying pressure on a weakness in your opponent's arm (anatomy).

Defensively, one of the best ways to control your partner's arm is by grabbing his wrist. When you block the wrist in certain defensive positions, you are not only blocking your opponent's arm but also his shoulder on that side **(see Figure 13).**

Figure 13

Famous attack moves, such as the Kimura and the Americana, are based on controlling your opponent's wrist. Grabbing your own wrist is also a great way to lock a good grip. *Guillotines*, some guard passes, and *bear hugs* are good examples. You can also grab your own wrist to defend against Kimura and counterattack your opponent.

For more examples on wrist techniques, go to

www.21BJJPrinciples.com and watch the complementary video of this chapter.

THE ELBOWS

The elbows should also be targeted for attack. Elbows are stronger than the wrist and fingers but weaker than the shoulders. For the most part, arm attacks (in one way or another) consist of manipulating your opponent's elbow. Straight arm-bars, Kimura's and Americana's are all good examples.

To better attack (or control) the elbows, we must move them away from our opponent's core. In my experience, the elbow weakens dramatically at any angle beyond 90 degrees from the upper body (**see Figure 14**).

The elbow is stronger the closer it is to the body. So one of our goals while attacking is to separate our opponent's elbows from the core of his body. Conversely, our elbows must always stay close to our core when defending.

Figure 14

Gaining More Leverage

In jiu-jitsu, we must always attack one of our opponent's limbs by using several parts of our body in combination to give us more leverage over our opponent. This principle works wonders when we are attacking our opponent's elbow.

Here are some examples:

We can use both of our arms against one of our opponent's elbows, bending it 90 degrees to attack (Kimura and Americana). To properly apply these submissions, we must use our legs, hips, and/or shoulders to gain more leverage. **Figure 15** is an example of an Americana lock.

Figure 15

To break our opponent's posture when he is on top in our guard, we can cup our opponent's elbows with our hands and pull them downwards while crunching our body, bringing our crossed legs to our chest **(see Figure 16)**.

Note: Breaking our opponent's posture is a great way to disrupt his offensive attacks.

Figure 16

Creative Ways to Use Our Elbows in Brazilian Jiu-Jitsu

Personally, I often use my elbows because my hands are usually busy making a strategic grip or serving as a point of balance for my body.

Here are a couple of very useful ways to use your elbows to both defend and attack your opponents.

1. Use your Elbows to get Rid of Undesirable Hooks.

Figure 17

When my opponent is stepping on my waist to push me away and create space, I use my elbows to remove his feet without committing other parts of my body (**see Figure 17**). You can also use your elbows to defend your back from hooks by pushing the hooks out when they are around your waist.

2. Use your Elbows to Control your Opponent's Hips

I can't stress enough the importance of controlling your opponent's hips at every moment of a match. You can use your elbows to control your opponent's hips from many positions. Side control, half guard, and guard passing are the most common.

Figure 18

For example, when passing the guard you can post your elbow on one side of your opponent's hips to pin his hips down into a flat position. This will help to gain more control over his motion (**see Figure 18**).

Posting your elbow on the mat next to your opponent's hips (when on top in side control or half guard) is another great way to gain control over him. It will help you to slow him down by partially blocking his hips (**see Figure 19**).

3. Use your Elbows to Block or Create Space

Figure 19

Many times the most efficient way to create space when defending your-self on the bottom is by using your elbows. Using your elbow to block your opponent's hips from moving forward, pushing his knees and fol-lowing up with hip escape, or putting your elbow on the base of your opponent's neck (between the trapezius and the neck) are great ways to stop your opponent in his tracks by creating more space for your defen-sive moves (e.g., guard recovery) (**see Figure 20**).

Figure 20

THE SHOULDERS

Using your shoulders is another excellent way to apply pressure on your opponent's body, and controlling your opponent's shoulders is a very useful way to restrict his body movement.

How to Apply Pressure with your Shoulders

You can use your shoulders to apply a considerable amount of pressure on your opponent when playing on top. Here are the most significant places on your opponent's body to apply shoulder pressure (when you have the opportunity, of course):

1. On your opponent's face;
2. On your opponent's hips; and
3. On your opponent's legs.

I'll elaborate more on these options. It is vital to your BJJ game that you thoroughly understand this principle.

Shoulder on the Face

Applying a shoulder on your opponent's face is a common method of control. If you are not currently using it properly, then you should consider starting right away.

When you apply pressure on your opponent's face, you force his face to the other side of your body, making it very difficult for him to turn his body toward you and hip escape away. Your opponent's defense is now limited. You can experiment with this principle by just simply asking someone to lay down with his/her face up. Then apply pressure on their face with your hand while pushing to one side of this person's body. While you are doing this, ask them to turn their body towards your hand. It's hard, right? Now imagine the increase in pressure when you are using your shoulder combined with a considerable amount of your weight.

You can use shoulder on the face pressure when you are passing the half guard, when you are controlling your opponent from the side, or when mounting him. (To watch a FREE video on how to use your shoulders on your opponent's face to add pressure and control, go to:
www.21BJJPrinciples.com)

Shoulder on the Hips

Again, I cannot stress this fact enough – controlling your opponent's hips is the single most important thing you can do to control your opponent's body.

When I say hips, I actually mean the pelvis bone. It's easier to visualize with the way is presented in **Figure 21**. As you can see in this picture, the hip is nothing more (and nothing less) than one piece of bone with a butterfly shape.

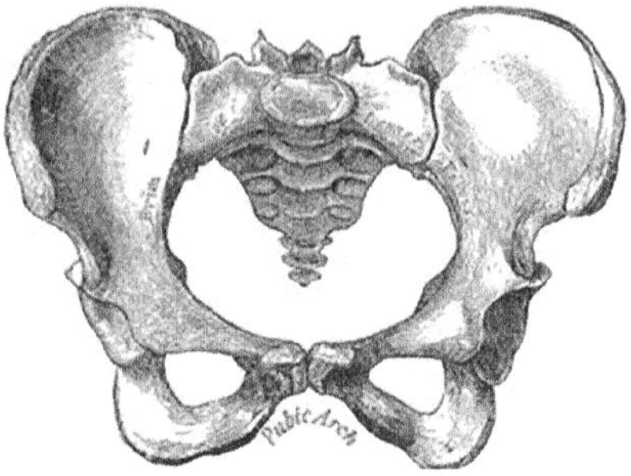

Figure 21

Why is it so important to control the hips?

Let's consider this scenario: Imagine you just hammered two long nails, one on each side of your opponent's pelvis to secure it in a flat position on the ground. Could your opponent then turn sideways, upside down, or hip escape? The answer is absolutely not!

Now that we know all the moves our opponent can execute involving hip movement, wouldn't it be awesome if we could just be sure that his hips were always flat against the mat?

In a jiu-jitsu match, it is very difficult to always keep your opponent's hips flat and unmovable. But if we focus on trying all the time, we are heading in the right direction.

Your shoulder is a great tool to use to control your opponent's pelvis (hips) because you can apply your weight pressure directly from your shoulder to one side of the pelvis (the side we don't want our opponent to move). Notice that I said shoulder, not shoulders. To apply the most weight pressure, you need to concentrate your pressure on one single point with the proper angle, using extra leverage by pushing from your toes (**see Figure 22**).

Figure 22

If you master this principle, you'll become a very undesirable person to train with because no one likes to be smashed or controlled on the bottom.

Shoulder on Legs

Your shoulders are also a really good way to apply pressure on your opponent's legs.

Once again, your pressure will maximize when you use only one of your shoulders to apply pressure. Combined with gravity and a little pushing from your feet, you can make yourself heavier than your opponent expects.

Why apply pressure on your opponent's legs?

The first reason (and in my opinion, the most important) is to wear your opponent out. If you are not consistently trying to wear your opponent out while engaging in Brazilian Jiu-Jitsu or any other style of self-defense match, you are 'rolling the dice'.

When your opponent is on the bottom defending his guard, his legs will be his first line of defense (and offense); therefore, it is extremely important for you to weaken his legs by applying your weight – in this case, with one of your shoulders.

The second reason is that you can use your shoulders to help you pin your opponent's legs down by pushing your shoulder onto his leg and letting your weight (and gravity) do the work.

One good way to control our opponent's legs (with one of your shoulders) while passing the guard is by pinning his legs sideways against the ground (or mat) by using your shoulder and body weight (what I call the chiropractor pass – **see Figure 23**).

Figure 23

The third reason is also very important: to defend. You can use your shoulders against the legs to defend from *hooks* and *submissions* (**see Figure 24**).

Figure 24

Defending Your Shoulders

Controlling the shoulders gives you more control over your opponent's body; therefore, defensively, you have to consistently focus on preventing your shoulders from being controlled.

Figure 25

Using your arms to block your opponent's attempt to control your shoulders **(Figure 25)** or hide them under your opponent's body **(Figure 26)** are great ways to defend your shoulders.

Figure 26

THE HEAD

In Jiu-Jitsu, you can use your head in many ways (other than thinking). You can also use your opponent's head to your advantage. I'll give you some examples.

Using your Opponent's Head to Increase Control

Let's return to the example about using your shoulder on our opponent's face. We've learned that when applying pressure on your opponent's head to push it to one side while on top limits his ability to move his hips.

I explained this principle when I wrote about shoulder pressure, but you can also use other parts of your body to control your opponent's head (see shoulder on the face). You can also use your head, hands, arms, butt, back, knees, and your thighs as well.

(To watch a FREE tutorial video, go to: **www.21BJJPrinciples.com**)

Using Your Head for Extra Balance

You can use your head as an extra hand or foot to keep your balance on top. Many times, when attempting to pass someone's guard and the Guard is really good, you'll need all the help you can get.

When your hands and feet are already busy either posted on the mat (or ground), grabbing something or being grabbed by your opponent, and you still need to regain (or maintain) your balance, the best choice is to use your head to do the job. How? By posting your forehead (or the crown of your head) on the mat and using it for balance.

In **Figure 27**, I show one example of how to improve your base by using your head. You can post your head on the ground when mounting your opponent, making your base stronger by using three points of balance instead of two.

Figure 27

Using your Head to Block your Opponent's Moves

Whenever possible, I use my head to block my opponent's moves. Notice that I said "whenever possible" because the opportunities are generally limited.

You don't want to be that guy or girl that uses his/her head to attempt blocking anything that comes in your direction. Why not? Because attached to your head is your neck, and your opponent (doesn't matter who he is) will choke you if you give him the chance.

So, how do I use my head to successfully block my opponent's moves without being caught? I only use this as a last resort, but there is a strategy that always works for me – defending from the butterfly guard.

This book is written to teach you principles of Brazilian jiu-jitsu so that you understand what is hidden behind the techniques, and are able to integrate these principles into your BJJ game (which is more important than ANY technique). Therefore, I won't explain all the specific techniques involved in defending your opponent's attacks from butterfly guard, but I will show you how to use your head to defend it.

One of the things you want to avoid when attempting to pass the butterfly guard is letting your opponent sit up the way he wants. There are three ways to keep an opponent from sitting up – by using your forearms, your head, or your body weight. Be aware that for each approach there are levels of risk.

Using a principle I've mentioned before – keeping your opponent's butt flat and (if possible) his back flat on the mat – provides the best defense against his sweep attempts. My favorite option is to keep my hips very heavy by sitting on my heels and making my body into a pyramid-like shape. This way I am applying a lot of weight to his feet, making it harder for him to lift me up to move me off balance.

Because I like to use this kind of body position, my body weight isn't available to flatten him out; therefore, I have to use my forearm or my head. I always try to use my forearm first, but sometimes my opponent is controlling my arms and then I have to use my head (**see Figure 28**).

Figure 28

You can watch a FREE tutorial video on how to use your head to defend from the butterfly guard by going to www.21BJJPrinciples.com.

> **Note:** When using your head to block, avoid leaning forward and losing good body position.

Using your Opponent's Head to Set up Attacks

For this principle, we have to go back to *action and reaction* – one of the most important principles of Brazilian jiu-jitsu, and maybe of all martial art styles. You can anticipate your opponent's next move if you *persuade* him to make it.

If you want him to raise his head and open more space (for arm-bars, double legs, etc.), you can often accomplish that by pulling his head downwards (most people will react by raising their head). Conversely, if you want his head closer to your hands to choke him, a good way to persuade him to help you is by pushing his head away.

THE FOOT

One of the biggest differences between jiu-jitsu and any other martial art style is the way jiu-jitsu fighters use their feet. In jiu-jitsu, your feet not only help to keep you in a standing position (or in balance) but also they must become your third and fourth hands. They become *hooks, forklifts*, a source of weight pressure, and many other things.

One of the most important subtle (and often overlooked) details in jiu-jitsu is the position of your feet during the match. They ALWAYS must be properly placed to get the most out of them. There are many examples of how to properly position your feet. In this book, I included some of the most significant ones. Unfortunately, there are so many things to talk about regarding proper foot position that I could write an entire book devoted to this subject.

Using your Feet to Apply Pressure

Using your feet to apply weight pressure is key. I'm a 170 lb. guy. One of the biggest compliments I consistently receive is that I feel like 300 lbs. when I am on top. I bet a lot of the good Black Belts who know how to maximize their weight receive similar compliments.

Why do Good Black Belts Feel so Heavy?

I've given you a lot of the reasons throughout this book, but one of them is the extra pressure applied when we use our toes (or feet) on the mat to push our bodies toward the area where we want to increase the pressure.

There is a very important connection between your feet pushing on the mat and extra pressure being applied on your opponent. Your body, with the help of gravity, can only be so heavy. To make yourself heavier, you need extra help. That little push coming from your feet can provide the extra help to make you feel heavier. This is one of the *invisible* techniques I talked about at the beginning of this book (**see Figure 29**).

Figure 29

Note: Let me remind you that I built a free website with video tutorials showing some of the principles and concepts presented in this book. All you have to do is go to **www.21BJJPrinciples.com** to check it out. You can also leave a comment or a question in case you need more information.

Using your Feet to Push, Pull or Block

In jiu-jitsu, your feet must be continually busy. One of the BIGGEST mistakes people make while defending their guard is forgetting to use their feet at all times.

Human beings use their hands more often than their feet, unless they are limited by a physical disability. Soccer and running track are two of a small number of sports where the feet are dominant. Because of this, we tend to forget to use our feet during a BJJ match or in a fight. This is a huge mistake and you will pay a price. Defending your guard by pushing, pulling, or blocking your opponent with your feet is a very effective strategy.

Why Should you use your Feet while Defending your Guard?

A jiu-jitsu match is a battle for conquering positions (fighting for inches). Usually, conquering great positions requires you to conquer parts of your opponent's body, and for that you need to close the gap between yourself and your opponent.

When defending your guard from your opponent's pressure and attacks, you can't allow him to close the gap the way he wants, and/or allow him to conquer significant parts of your body. Also, when defending your guard, you always want your opponent off balance to facilitate your sweep and submission attempts.

Once I read the quote, "Nothing happens until something moves." This applies perfectly to a BJJ match.

So using your feet to push (or pull) your opponent can force him to move his body where you want him to go, improving both your leverage and the opportunity to predict his next move. Using your feet to block your opponent is another great way to stop him in his tracks and prevent him from closing the gap on you. Remember: You must always control the distance between you and your opponent.

To push or block your opponent with your foot, you have to use the sole of your foot; to pull, you use more of the top part of your foot, hooking on to some part of your opponent.

Using your feet to Hip Escape and Bridge

Two of the most important Brazilian jiu-jitsu defensive moves are the bridge (or 'Upa') and the hip escape; the leverage for these moves comes from your feet.

Figure 30

I mention this because the role your feet have on those two very important Brazilian jiu-jitsu moves is often overlooked. I've seen people trying to hip escape by using the leverage from their arms (**see Figure 30**). That's not only the wrong way but also the most tiring way. Your legs are much stronger than your arms. At all times you should be focusing on using your legs and feet more than your arms and hands (**see Figure 31**).

Figure 31

THE SHIN

I always tell my students, "Your shin is your shield." This analogy works for any position.

Some time ago, I was watching a documentary about the Spartans and their famous battle against the Persians. I learned that the Spartans were really good with using their shields to both defend and attack. This skill was one of the reasons they were very hard to beat (besides the fact that they had been groomed to be fearless warriors).

Earlier, I mentioned the *Braveheart* analogy. In my opinion, this is an extremely important principle of jiu-jitsu. Using the movie's battles as an example, I explained the reasons you should face your fears each time when sparring, and always engage with your opponent like they did in the movie (see chapter 6).

So, What Does all this have to do with your Shin?

Jiu-jitsu is a battle between you and your opponent, and I believe that when passing someone's guard (or defending yours), you should always use your shin as your shield. Most of the time, your upper body should be positioned slightly behind your shins, only opening to attack.

Obviously, there will be times when your upper body will be ahead of your shins (e.g., passing the half guard or butterfly guard), but even then you should still try to figure out ways to use your shins. I am a big believer of this principle, and I've built almost my whole Brazilian jiu-jitsu game based on it.

More Examples of how to use your Shin

Passing the Guard

When you are in the process of passing someone's guard, you should use your shin to apply pressure on your opponent's hamstrings. To accomplish this, you must be standing in a squat position (**see Figure 32**) with the pressure leg slightly in front of the leverage leg (I say leverage leg because it is the leg responsible for pushing the other forward). Every time both of your feet are in what the wrestlers call 'square stance', you lose the front shin pressure.

Figure 32

In this position, your shin can also work as a windshield wiper to defend yourself against inconvenient hooks applied by your opponent. The De La Riva hook is a good example of a hook you want to avoid, and you can do that by properly using your shin – moving it outwards in a 90-degree angle (**see Figure 33**).

Figure 33

Again referring to passing your opponent's guard, you can use your shin to pin one of your opponent's legs down by kneeling on it. This way you neutralize one of his legs, temporarily giving you one less thing to worry about (**see Figure 34**).

Figure 34

The *Shin Slicer Pass* is another great way to use your shin to pass someone's guard (**see Figure 35**).

Figure 35

Defending your Guard

Putting your shin between your body and your opponent is a very effective way to block an opponent from passing your guard. There are different angles that will fit different purposes. Once again the motion is very similar to a windshield wiper. Sometimes you will have to block somewhere close to the chest and shoulders; sometimes you will have to block the hips and legs.

Refer to **Figure 36**, where I illustrate an example of how you can use your shin to defend your guard.

Figure 36

Using your Shin to Prevent Submissions

One of the major defensive moves that can be used to prevent you from being caught in guard submissions (such as arm-bar, triangle, or omoplata) is to post your elbows on your thighs (**check the position of my elbows in Figure 37**) while having your shin slightly ahead of your elbows. This

Figure 37

action closes the gap that your opponent needs to move his hips closer to your upper body, taking away his most threatening angle for leverage.

THE HIPS

I've discussed the concept of the hips as the center of your 'board' and the most important spot on your body to be controlled. But can you also use your own hips to your advantage? The answer is YES!

Your hips are an excellent defense 'tool' because they provide weight pressure to control your opponent.

While passing your opponent's guard, your **primary** focus should be on making your hips heavy, unless you want to try something more acrobatic (which doesn't work for most of the older people). On the other hand, when defending your guard you should focus on keeping your hips free and moving.

> **Remember:** Your opponent wants to control your hips, and it is your mission to prevent him from doing so. Hip escape and other moves that involve moving your hips are vital to completing this mission.

Using your Hips to Control your Opponent

Remember that using your hips to apply pressure (to control your opponent's hips) is probably one of the most powerful ways to maintain proper control in almost any position.

Let me give you some examples:

When controlling my opponent from the top in side control, I use my hips to apply pressure on him in key spots. If I am using the cross face control, I push the side of my hips against my opponent's hips to keep him from hip escaping from me (**see Figure 38**).

Figure 38

When mounting my opponent, I apply more weight on one side of my opponent's hips – usually the opposite side from where I want him to turn – because I would rather be heavier on one side of his body than light on both (**see Figure 39**).

Figure 39

I also use my hips to increase weight and pressure when controlling with my knee on the belly (we say knee on the belly, but it is actually whole shin on the belly). I accomplish this by sitting on the heel of the leg that is pressing into my opponent's body (**see Figure 40**).

Figure 40

Using your Hips to Defend

Another great time to use your hips is when defending. You can use the back of your hips (butt) to bump your opponent away from your body in order to create space. You can use your hips by bridging, or you can hip escape to change angles. You can also move them up and down, or rock them. Your ability to move your hips will define your agility in BJJ.

Using your Hips to Attack

When it comes down to attacking, using your hips is extremely import-ant. You have to continuously move your hips to create different angles of attack. Some effective ways to use your hips to create different angles that will catch your opponent off guard include hip escape, moving your hips upside down, and moving your hips forward and backward, up and down, under your opponent, etc.

HANDS

It makes sense that using your hands should be the easiest concept to grasp. Although there are ways to maximize how you use your hands against your opponent, there are also ways to mess it up. In Jiu-Jitsu, you use your hands to set up attacks, grab, cup, push, pull, block, post, and choke your opponent.

You need to know where and how to properly use your hands for maximum benefit. Correctly using your hands helps to conserve energy, and achieve the results you desire.

Take grips for example. It is very important to grab your opponent's kimono or body on the right spot and in the right way. There are certain grips to avoid because they waste too much energy and don't get the job done. My advice to you is to pay close attention to someone's grips while they are executing a good technique, and then try to understand why they are there and not somewhere else.

When it comes to pushing and blocking, there are key places on your body that provide better leverage than others. For instance, it is better to push (or block) by posting your hands on the shoulder, hips, head, and wrist than to push (or block) the chest, rib cage, belly, etc.

Once again, this book is not intended to show all the grips (or all the places) you should put your hands (for that you have your instructor) but to help you understand that gripping and posting your hands properly will make your techniques more successful while conserving valuable energy.

Chapter 13

The Grandmaster Helio Gracie Principle

> 66 To secure ourselves against defeat lies in our own hands, but the opportunity of defeating the enemy is provided by the enemy himself. 99
>
> —Sun Tzu

Our great Grandmaster Helio Gracie and the great Chinese general, Sun Tzu – author of *The Art of War*–used the same principle to defeat their opponents.

One of the Grandmaster's most famous quotes was, "If you don't lose, you win!" This highlights the emphasis he consistently put on the importance of defense in developing the whole jiu-jitsu system. Grandmaster Helio's #1 rule was "protect yourself at all times". Brazilian jiu-jitsu is the perfect self-defense, and we should use it to defend ourselves from any physical attack. "When you fight someone bigger and stronger than you, if you survive, you are the victor!" said Master Helio.

The perfect defense allows the BJJ fighter to rest more than his opponent, remain calm in looking for opportunities to counterattack, and conserve energy while their opponent wastes his on unsuccessful attempts to attack.

This principle has been lost along the way at various BJJ academies whose focus has become solely to win Brazilian jiu-jitsu competitions, not to be able to defend themselves in a street fight (for example).

Why has *Grandmaster Helio Gracie* developed his jiu-Jitsu strategy around defense?

Grandmaster Helio was a skinny guy (about 147 lbs.). He knew that he couldn't rely on strength to defeat an opponent (very rarely was he stronger than his opponents). So his idea was to wear his opponents out by letting them waste energy trying to attack him without success. Then when they were gassed, he would submit them and force them to quit.

So then comes the big question: How can you properly use this principle while you are fighting?

Here is some advice you should follow in order to conserve your energy:

- Defense always comes first;
- Always look for a comfortable position where you don't waste energy;
- Be patient – keep your wits;
- Don't persist in a position that has been lost;
- Always look for weaknesses in your opponent's position;
- Learn when to improve your position, and when to retreat;
- Develop at least one good escape for each attack; and
- Know when to attack and submit.

Properly following the guidance above will get you much further in any fighting situation. I strongly recommend you take a day or two during your week of BJJ training to focus only on these steps until you fully absorb them. **They are the essence of our jiu-jitsu.**

Chapter 14

The New Shiny Object Syndrome

In business there is a term called 'The New Shiny Object Syndrome', which I first heard from Dan Kennedy, a marketing and business guru.

He believes that one of the major problems every business owner faces is losing sight of mastering the basics while focusing instead on the continual pursuit of the newest shiny object (or new trend).

Owners often stop working on what first made their business successful – all the core things they did to build and improve their business. Instead, they focus on the 'latest and greatest' approach to marketing, or chase the latest technology.

Dan says there is nothing wrong with keeping up-to-date on new trends, but a new trend comes along almost every month. So, if you focus your efforts on chasing every new trend, you will neither succeed nor master anything.

Unfortunately, I've noticed that in BJJ we have the same syndrome. I have students that have a one-month focus on deep half guard, and then the next month they are focusing on 50/50, and then the next month... (you get the picture). Yet, they don't know how to properly escape back control or mount position, which are the core basics of any BJJ game.

This syndrome doesn't just happen in my academy, it happens in BJJ academies around the world and you may be suffering from it at this very moment.

Ask yourself this question:

Do I know exactly how to properly escape from mount or back control, knee on belly, side control, arm-bars, chokes, triangles, omoplatas, Americanas and Kimuras?

If the answer is no (or maybe), then stop focusing on whatever you're currently focused on, and dedicate at least the next two months to working on escaping those positions. After a minimum of two months, ask yourself the same question again. When your answer turns to yes, congratulations! Now you can go back to your prior area of focus.

Chapter 15

The Big Rock Analogy

I learned this analogy from one of the Ribeiro brothers (either Saulo, or Xande), but I don't remember exactly which one. What I remember is how much sense it made to me when transferred to my Jiu-Jitsu game. The analogy was to imagine that someone just threw a big rock on top of your body, what would be your first reaction? I believe pushing or blocking the rock so that it doesn't continue hurting your body, right?

Well, in jiu-jitsu, a lot of people do the opposite. They grab the rock or give the rock a big hug. I can't count the number of times I have seen BJJ students, when their opponent has just passed their guards, using all their energy to grab their opponent instead of blocking him or pushing him away. It's like grabbing the big rock.

When your opponent has achieved a major control position against you (for example, side control or mount), you don't want to pull his weight against your body because you will sabotage yourself. You want to make room to escape. Remember, push the big rock away from you.

I have another question: When you want to push this big rock away from you to be free again, would you push this rock upwards? Sideways?

If you push upwards, we know that gravity will push the rock right back at you. So when pushing your opponent to create room for your escape, don't push him upward – push him sideways!

Don't ever try to fight against gravity – you will always lose. Now let's imagine the rock is too heavy to be pushed; now what would you do? Instead of trying to push the rock away from you, why not just block the rock and scoot away from it? The same idea is applied for BJJ – block and hip escape.

Still using the same analogy, imagine the rock is smashing you and you need to create space between you and it. Which part of your body would give you more leverage, your legs or your arms? If your answer is the legs, you are completely right. This is why bridging is so important (if you are unfamiliar with a bridge, please ask your BJJ instructor to explain). When your opponent is too tight (or heavy) and you can't block and hip escape, you will have to bridge for the space to initiate your next move.

Remember: It's a battle for inches and sometimes even a fraction of an inch.

Chapter 16

The Fine Line

Grandmaster Helio Gracie said, "From the moment any technique starts until the moment that it ends, there will be one split of second that it will have a weakness." I call this weakness 'The Fine Line'. People say, "There is a fine line between coincidence and fate." In jiu-jitsu, there is a fine line between being too early and being too late. Before our opponent crosses this line, it's too early to react, and after the line has been crossed, it's too late.

It is very important for the BJJ fighter to act immediately – precisely at the point when their opponent reaches this line. This fine line can also be referred to as timing, and it comes in many different shapes and forms. It is important to identify this fine line when you are attacking, and when you are defending. A good number of BJJ practitioners let their opponents cross this line many times during matches, continually putting themselves in bad positions.

In order to master Brazilian jiu-jitsu, you must know exactly where this line is on every move. Consequently, you will be switching from your offensive mode immediately back to defense or counterattack mode. You may even switch attacks before your opponent crosses the line to establish his position.

This highlights the importance of the fine line. I dare say that when we miss it, it is the major cause of our defeat.

There are four major actions you must follow when the fine line presents itself:

1. Learn when your position is lost and then immediately start a transition to the next best option;

2. Learn when to retreat instead of wasting your energy struggling to advance (or maintain) a bad position;
3. Counter attack at the precise moment your opponent reaches the line; and
4. Make a move to improve your position before your opponent cross the line.

Learn When your Position is Lost and Immediately Start the Transition to the Next Best Option

I can best explain this by illustrating a very common example. Imagine you are attacking your opponent from his back. You have both hooks (feet) around his waist and are now trying to choke him. He defends the attack and starts to put his back against the ground (mat). Without acknowledging his defense, you insist on trying to get the submission from the back, consequently losing your back control and ending up in his guard. This is a common example of failing to identify the fine line, and letting your opponent cross it.

At the moment that you feel that your opponent is about to escape, why not switch from back control to mount control before the opponent's escape is completed? This allows you to transition into the next best position while avoiding the fall into a bad one.

The example above is just one of many situations you will face. Use this principle when you are attempting submission A and then switch to submission B, or when you attempt escape A and then need to switch to escape B. Any time you are using one technique that is not working at that exact moment, you should switch immediately to something else.

Learn when to Retreat Instead of Wasting your Energy Struggling to Advance or Maintain a Bad Position

BJJ is like a human chess game. You must use strategic moves to attack and achieve the submission while not forgetting that your defense is vulnerable (and open for your opponent's counterattacks). Remember, your opponent also wants to control you into a submission position.

We're often so focused on the attack that all that comes to our mind is, "I need to get something quick before he has a chance to get me." But this type of thinking is 'putting all your eggs in one basket'. If you drop the basket, you know what happens…you lose. Our focus on defense must be equal to our focus on the attack. I'm being repetitive by saying this, but I can't stress it enough.

For example, imagine your opponent is stuck in a triangle from your guard but isn't tapping. He is starting to twist his body and gets you almost on your side, but you're still holding his head with all your effort, squeezing like there is no tomorrow.

He is still not tapping and is about to slip out of your triangle to land right at your side, but you are still squeezing him. You've exhausted yourself by squeezing too long; he escapes and lands on your side. Now he is controlling you in a side control choke (for example). You are so tired that you tap right away.

Sound familiar? All of us at one point in our BJJ careers are guilty of this big mistake. I hope after reading this chapter that you'll stop making this mistake (if guilty). Alter your strategy to focus on figuring out when the fine line will appear, and when it is time to retreat. Do what BJJ masters do – switch modes before it is too late.

Counterattack Right at the Moment your Opponent Reaches the Line

As I mentioned earlier in this chapter, the fine line can also be called timing. This is a perfect example of timing. Timing is moving exactly at the right time; in BJJ it's when you can use your opponent's power (energy) combined with yours to maximize the power of your move.

When I say power, I'm referring to strength, motion, balance, or speed. It can be one of these or a combination of two or more. If you want to save your energy and outlast, executing the techniques at the right time is a must.

Let me give you an example to illustrate this principle when you are on the bottom and your opponent is controlling you on side control.

He is super tight, making it impossible for you to escape. You try some bridge attempts without success. What now? You only have one wise option – wait until your opponent moves and react quickly by bridging right at the moment he starts his motion. This way you will use his energy (action) against him. But you must bridge to the direction he is moving, otherwise you will go 'against the flow'. This is one way of using this principle.

Make a Move to Improve your Position Before your Opponent Crosses the Line

There are many situations where you can apply this principle, but to do so you must first understand the concept.

So, let's imagine your opponent is about to pass your guard. You've tried everything in your power to stop it from happening, but it's happening anyway. If you let your opponent complete his move and then try to defend it afterwards, you are already late. He has crossed the fine line. You will be exactly where he wants you, and typically you'll be exposed to his subsequent attacks. What should you do instead to stay ahead of the game? Position your body in such a way that it will be easier to escape from side control before he completes his control position. In this case, turn your body slightly sideways to prepare it for a hip escape or the turtle position.

The same applies when your opponent is about to lock any kind of submission or establish any kind of control. When you feel you cannot stop it from happening, prepare for the next move instead of continuing to fight a lost fight. This will give you a head start on the next play of the game.

Now, go get to work.

Chapter 17

Energy Management

This is the most important of all principles and is overlooked by many Brazilian Jiu-Jitsu practitioners. In a fight, what happens to the guy who becomes exhausted first? If you've ever been involved in any kind of fight, sparring, or BJJ roll, you know that the first person to become exhausted loses. You don't want to be the guy who tires first, right? You know what happens to him.

So this is a 'no-brainer' – you have to conserve your energy just enough to outlast your opponent. How? We'll get into that, but first let me tell you a quick story that will help illustrate this concept.

A few weeks ago while reading the *Gracie* magazine, I came across an interview with two very accomplished athletes in Brazilian jiu-jitsu and Judo, Ronaldo Jacare and Flavio Canto. Both of them have notoriously aggressive games on the ground (they are very submission driven), which means that when they see it, they give their all to get it. They were talking about the 'nimble game', which they consider to be the best way to play the game.

If you are unfamiliar with the 'nimble game', in a nutshell it consists of always keeping the fight flowing at a good pace. You consistently move quickly, ready to connect to your next best move, always keeping your eyes open to any submission opportunity that might pass in front of you. When you see it, you go for it. Sounds like fun, right?

I've known Jacare and Flavio for a long time, and I use this kind of style in many of my training sessions. I believe it opens your mind to many more possibilities, and makes your game more versatile. However, I don't think this is for everybody. Also, I don't think it's the only way to become more technical or to master Brazilian jiu-jitsu.

This chapter is about energy management. Ronaldo "Jacare" and Flavio are professional athletes; they have been since they were teenagers. They train two to three times a day, plus cross-train by doing a bunch of physical exercises with the help of a personal trainer. They are a different species! Not all BJJ practitioners can dedicate their whole day to keep up with their pace. If you can, great!

As I was writing this book, I turned forty years old and I have had 26 years of Brazilian jiu-jitsu training. Even though I maintain a very healthy lifestyle with daily BJJ training and a workout routine, it is hard for me to always be in my best shape and even harder to keep up with the physical condition of those two guys. Now, let's imagine Ronaldo "Jacare" comes to my academy today (as I write this book, Jacare is 3rd in the UFC in his weight division), and asks me to train with him. Because I like the nimble game, let's imagine we both engage in it. At this moment, he is in peak physical condition and I am only following my daily routine. Who do you think is going to run out of gas first?

> **A little advice:** You must never run out of gas before your opponent.

If I play my nimble game against his nimble game, I won't be able to keep up with his pace, and I will consequently run out of gas. As good BJJ practitioners, we know what happens when we run out of gas, right?

You must be thinking, "How can I outlast my opponent if he seems to be in better physical condition than me?" This is when energy management comes into play. Everything in this book is correlated because we are talking about Brazilian jiu-jitsu principles that never change, and they are all correlated as a whole.

In Brazilian Jiu-Jitsu, or Gracie Jiu-Jitsu (one and the same), the core objective is to have the opportunity to survive against ANY opponent. And for that… you must at least outlast your opponent. This is how important energy management is to your game. Applying all the principles of this book is vital to your energy management, but you have to add two more things: breathing correctly and proper mindset.

Without breathing properly and without the right mindset, you won't outlast your opponent even if you apply all the principles of this book. This is why it is essential to understand these two principles and apply them to your game starting today.

Breathing Properly

If you have practiced and watched jiu-jitsu for as long as I have, you've probably noticed that many people don't breathe properly while training. Some barely breathe at all – like they are fighting underwater… or something.

Also, a lot of people only breathe through their mouths, sucking the air in but not using their lungs at full capacity. If you are guilty of one (or more) of these breathing sins, then today is your lucky day! I will teach you how to properly breathe, and that alone will boost your endurance 100%.

> **Note:** If you have been breathing inefficiently for a long time, you won't be able to change your breathing immediately. Breathing is a habit, and to destroy a bad habit takes a little bit of effort. But the good news is that today is the best day to start.

How to Breathe Properly During a BJJ Match

Your first step to breathing properly is to focus on pushing the air out through your mouth or nose instead of sucking in the air. Inhalation will come naturally after a complete exhalation, without any need to suck air back in.

> **Tip:** Make sounds when you are exhaling so you can hear it happening until you get used to it. I still make noises when I exhale. It helps me keep track of my breathing throughout the fight.

The second step is to ALWAYS inhale through your nose. The third step is to use your diaphragm (the large muscle between your lungs and your stomach) instead of the upper part of your lungs only. Compare lungs with a balloon. When you blow up a balloon, the balloon fills up from the bottom to the top; so do our lungs. The majority of people have never breathed with the bottom part of their lungs, thus they have never used their lungs to their full capacity. If that sounds crazy or impossible to you, you can watch a free video on this website: **www.21BJJPrinciples.com** – I will teach you how to do it, or you can sign up for yoga classes, where they also will teach you how to breathe properly.

> **Note:** Not all yoga studios teach their students how to breathe properly – look for Hatha Yoga classes.

Proper Mindset

If you have followed my instructions on how to breathe and are now controlling your breath more efficiently, then it will be easier to control your mind as well (because they are both linked). When I talk about mindset, I'm telling you to keep your wits at all times, and you can only do that if you remain calm even when under pressure.

In general, a good way to calm yourself is by focusing on your breathing. Exhale more, and for a longer period of time. You have to control your excitement, your anxieties, and your fears. No matter who you are or your level of jiu-jitsu, you will feel one or more of these emotions at times. If we don't, we will lose positions, fall into submission attempts, and we won't think clearly about our next best move.

Most of our emotions result from our minds either dwelling on past experiences or looking into the future. The thing is, when we are in a BJJ match, we are living the present at its full capacity and nothing else matters. This is a wonderful experience and we have to take full advantage of it by keeping our mind at all times in the present. By keeping your mind in the moment, you'll be able to make better decisions without fearing the future (which clouds our judgment of the present).

Only through a mix of experience of training in BJJ and the use of the principles in this book, will you be able to control your emotions. But remember! You must control emotions to the best of your ability – at ALL TIMES. One little slip can jeopardize everything you had accomplished during a match.

The Correct Tactic

The correct tactic for an excellent performance combined with energy management (they are correlated) is knowing exactly when to switch from a tighter position to a more explosive move (or moves); when to relax and when to use strength; and when to make the transition from a closely formed body defensive position to using a specific part of the body to execute the task you want.

Chapter 18

The Real Estate Analogy

You might be thinking, "What does real estate have to do with Brazilian jiu-jitsu?" Well, if you've been reading this book, by now you're aware that I use some unconventional analogies. Once explained, I hope they make sense and help you better understand (and retain) the concepts and principles of BJJ.

What is the most valuable real estate on our body? Knowing the answer will be extremely helpful when defending and attacking.

If you don't want to get submitted (and I believe you don't!), you must not leave your neck, arms, legs, feet, knees, or hands unprotected against an attack by your opponent. You will give him an immediate victory (if he is good at Jiu-Jitsu). So these are the most valuable pieces of 'real estate' on your body; if you give them away, you lose. It probably sounds obvious to protect these parts of your body, but BJJ students regularly expose at least one of them to submission attacks.

Although the body parts mentioned above are the most important ones to protect, there are other pieces of 'real estate' that people take for granted – the area from your waist to your shoulders, for instance.

This part of the body is related to all kinds of controlling positions, and by now we know that controlling our opponent is a great way to get the submission (on the other hand, getting controlled by our opponent is a great way to lose the fight). So, if control is so important and the second most sought out part of our body to be controlled is from our waist to our shoulders, I dare say we must protect this 'piece of real estate' at all times.

There are two very effective ways to defend this part of your body, and in my opinion, you cannot become a master of Brazilian jiu-jitsu without knowing how to defend it well.

In real life, if you don't want one of your most valuable pieces of real estate taken (or bought), you either surround it with a big, impenetrable wall for protection, or you offer it for an obnoxiously large amount of money (way over the value), or you don't sell. In a BJJ fight, take the 'don't sell' out of the equation because, like it or not, it is there to be 'sold' or 'taken'.

So your only two options are to sell for an obnoxious amount of money (which in your BJJ match translates to you putting a lot of energy and perseverance into defending it until your opponent gives up trying), or build a big impenetrable wall (which consists of closing the gap at all times). I personally like the last option because it conserves more of my energy.

How to Close the Gap

To close this gap you have to use your elbows. If you lower your elbows and bring your same side knee up, and connect them both, you've built a wall (**see Figure 41**).

Figure 41

You can also connect your elbows to your pelvis. I believe that if most people drop their elbows down – almost as if they are putting their elbows into their pants pockets – their elbows will naturally connect to their pelvis bone. Now, if you bring your knees towards your chest as you drop your elbow down, then you will create a very solid and effortless wall – one that is really hard to penetrate (**see Figure 42**).

Figure 42

Chapter 19

How to Maximize your Weight Pressure

In this book, I give many tips on how to make you feel heavier while on top in a ground fight, or in a BJJ/grappling match. Because I consider it such an important topic, and an *immutable* principle of Brazilian jiu-jitsu, I decided to devote a complete chapter to it.

Earlier I mentioned how satisfying it is to hear a training partner say, "Man, you feel like 300lbs!" I love this kind of compliment (and I get it quite often). It means I am using my weight pressure (remember the 7 P's) properly. The reason I am able to make my body feel heavy on top is only because I apply all the rules in this book in unison. So what is the secret to making a 170 lbs. body feel like 200-300 lbs.?

There are a couple of 'rules of thumb' for proper weight pressure. Here they are:

Rule #1: Pick a side.

What I mean by that is you have to decide if you are going to put more weight on your right or your left side.

Remember, if your weight is spread out evenly, 50% comes from the left part of your body and 50% comes from the right. If you weigh 170 lbs. (and let's assume for this example that you will use all your weight at all times), then you will be using 85 lbs. on each side, right?

Now, restating an earlier example, let's imagine that you decide to apply more weight on your right side – maybe 60% of your weight. Now it is no longer 85 lbs.; it becomes 102 lbs. You are using 17 extra pounds on that side. Those extra 17 lbs. can really help if your goal is to control that part of your opponent's body (or smash that side more, for defensive purposes).

Rule #2: Use your hands and/or feet to help increase your weight.

Gravity can only make you so heavy. If you weigh 170 lbs., for instance, and if you could use all your weight (physically impossible), then you will only feel like you weigh 170 lbs. But why do some people feel so much heavier than they are?

One reason is because they use their hands and/or their feet to direct their weight to the desired point. So, pick a side and use your feet and/or hands to push from the mat to direct your weight onto the side you pick, thereby increasing weight pressure on your opponent. You can also pull your partner toward your body while putting your weight on him – just be careful not to waste too much energy doing so.

Rule #3: Don't tense your body.

I explained the importance of relaxing your body on top and refraining from being stiff like plywood (chapter 3). Relaxing your body – not completely, but just enough to be firm and not stiff – is a great way to maximize your weight.

Chapter 20

Limbs vs. Limbs Principle

There is a principle that when implemented properly, elevates your BJJ game by simply being logical.

Make it an even fight! We tend to use our hands too much against all parts of our opponent's body. Obviously, your hands are weaker than your legs, upper body, hips, and shoulders. Be logical; don't use your hands to fight against stronger parts of your opponent's anatomy. You are fighting an uneven fight. You need to even it out more in order to succeed, but how?

The secret is to use your legs to fight your opponent's legs; hips to fight his hips; shoulders to fight his shoulders, etc. It doesn't necessarily mean it has to always be that way, but this is definitely the preferred method.

Once you learn how to use this principle, it is time to make the fight uneven – but now you are on the strong side of the rope. For example, you can use your legs to fight the legs, and then add your hand and your shoulder to the equation. The idea is to always have more leverage than your opponent, not less.

Chapter 21

The Base Principle

This is the last and perhaps one of the most important principles in this book.

First, what is base? Webster's Dictionary has many definitions for base, but the most relevant one for us is: *the bottom of something considered as its support*: **FOUNDATION.**

In BJJ, base is what supports your moves when you are on your feet (standing), or on top of your opponent. Base is likewise the *foundation* of all the standing BJJ self-defense techniques, and all moves you perform when on top in a fight.

Having a great base is almost equivalent to having a great balance. The image of a triangle is a good representative of the Brazilian jiu-jitsu base. Look carefully to the silhouette of **Figures 43 and 44**. Do you see the triangle shape? **Figure 43** shows the knee on belly control and **Figure 44** is a standard standing BJJ base that is the beginning of upcoming techniques.

Figure 43

A good base is what will protect you from being taken down, or from being swept – guarding you from being on the bottom against your will. Even though BJJ has many great attacks and defenses from the bottom, we have to fight our opponent's weight when in that position.

Figure 44

Many BJJ masters have developed their base and agility to such a level that they appear to move like cats when fighting on top. I've mentioned in this book a quote from the legendary Sun Tzu, which expresses, in my opinion, how a BJJ master should approach a fight, **"Move swift as the Wind and closely-formed as the Wood. Attack like Fire and be still as the Mountain."** Notice that he said, "… still as the Mountain." What better than a mountain to illustrate the idea of an excellent base?!

Black Belt Tips: The fear of getting swept, taken down, or losing balance is a major obstacle to an outstanding base. Lose the fear! Imagine that you are a cat and someone is trying to force your back into a bucket of water (don't try this experiment at home if you have cats!). What would the cat do? It would do its best to always fall on its paws. Also, make sure you have at least one part of your body solidly planted on the ground to be your support (like my foot in Figure 43) and one part of the body ready to post if you need it.

What insight can you take from this chapter? How about…develop the Base Principle in order to master BJJ, unless you want to be that guy that only fights from his guard and is always scared to be on top of his opponent. Having a good base will take a lot of training, but applying the principles of this book will help you get there faster.

Final Thoughts

Now that you've read all the chapters in this book (at least I hope you did), your next move should be to analyze your own Brazilian Jiu-Jitsu game while comparing to the principles taught here.

Depending on your level at this moment, you might be using many (or all) of these principles already (or maybe not). Look deep into your game and try to identify the ones you are already using and the ones you are not. Then pick one you are not currently using, and apply it immediately to your game, until you have mastered them all one by one.

If you are new in Brazilian jiu-jitsu – great! The knowledge in this book will help you accelerate your learning curve and give you a strong sense of the core principles that will never change. To reinforce this knowledge, come back to this book at least once a year.

Why Did I Use Analogies?

I believe analogies will help you retain the information in this book by creating a mental picture of something common in your life, and then relating that thought to your BJJ game.

Most of the analogies in this book are mine, but the ones told to me I've never forgotten. My wish is that you never forget them, and will pass them along one day to someone else (and maybe even make your own analogies). For me, the core of Brazilian Jiu-Jitsu has a lot to do with the day-to-day situations in our lives. The way we approach BJJ is relatable to the way we approach our lives. Take a moment to think about that.

My intention in writing this book is to enrich the way Brazilian jiu-jitsu students see our art. I hope the principles and concepts presented in this book are as beneficial to you as they have been to me.

So I hope you enjoyed it, and are taking full advantage of everything this book has to offer (including your free access to **www.21BJJPrinciples.com**, where you can watch videos explaining the principles in this book).

Sensei Paulo Guillobel

Made in United States
Orlando, FL
24 April 2022